FOOTSTEPS
IN TIME

THE
Romans

Sally Hewitt

Contents

3000 BC	2000 BC	1000 BC	0	1000 AD	2000 AD

Egyptians

Greeks

Romans

Vikings

CHILDRENS PRESS ®

CHICAGO

Who were the Romans?

The Romans came from the ancient city of Rome. Legends tell how twin brothers, Romulus and Remus, were thrown into the Tiber River by their wicked uncle. A wolf rescued them and took care of them. When they grew up, they built the city of Rome, and Romulus became its first king.

Great Britain

London

Germany

France

Spain

Rome

Italy

Mediterranean Sea

Syria

Egypt

The Romans became very powerful and conquered the countries surrounding them. The ruler of the whole Roman Empire was called the emperor.

The people of the Roman Empire were divided into three groups. Roman citizens could vote in elections and serve in the army. Noncitizens could not vote. Slaves had no freedom and were owned by citizens.

Roman sandals

Outdoors, Romans wore leather boots tied with thongs.
Indoors, they wore sandals.

You will need:

Cardboard   Hole punch

Two long pieces of string, or very long shoelaces

Follow the steps . . .

1. Stand on the cardboard and draw an outline of your feet. Cut out the shapes you have drawn.

2. Punch holes around the edges of the foot shapes.

3. Sit down and put your feet on the sandals. One at a time, thread the laces through the holes and over your feet.

Bracelets

Romans believed that if they wore a snake bracelet they would live a long life.

You will need:

White paper	Thin cardboard	Tape
Gold paint	Scissors	Pencil

Follow the steps . . .

1. Twist a long rectangle of white paper round and round. Cut it to fit around your wrist.

2. Draw snake heads on cardboard. Cut them out and tape them onto each end of the twisted paper.

3. Paint the bracelets with gold paint and let them dry. Make or paint eyes on the snake heads.

4. You could try making brooches too.

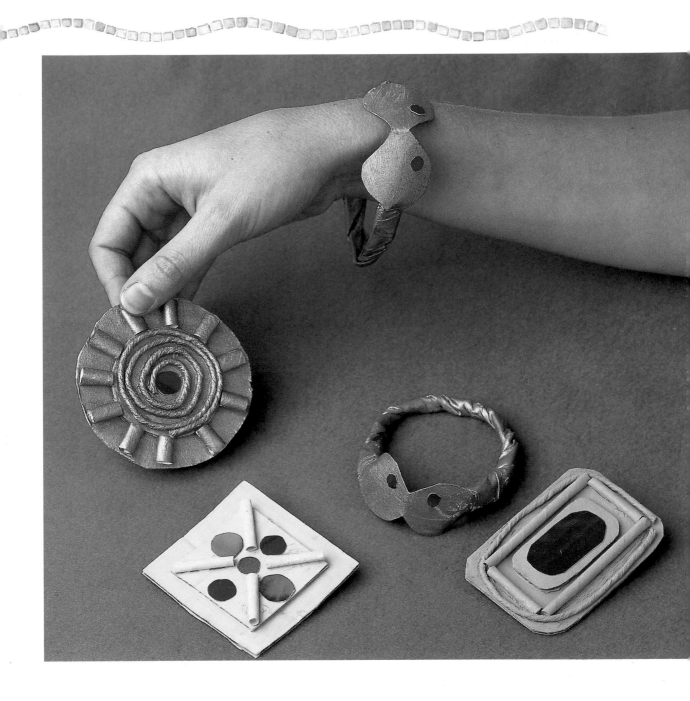

Life in a Roman town

Walls with gates were built around Roman towns to keep them safe from attack. Two main roads entered the gates and crossed the town from north to south and from east to west.

The busy marketplace in the center was surrounded by stores and public buildings. People swarmed into the theater and amphitheater for entertainment, and visited the public baths. They built temples to the gods.

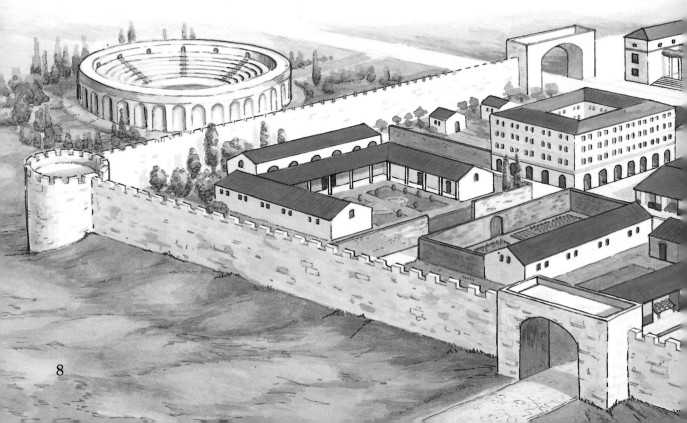

A *domus* was a private house owned by rich people. It had many rooms set around an open courtyard. Slaves did all the housework.

Insulae were apartment buildings up to five stories high. Water was carried from fountains, and waste was thrown out of the windows. There were no kitchens, so people bought hot meals from street vendors.

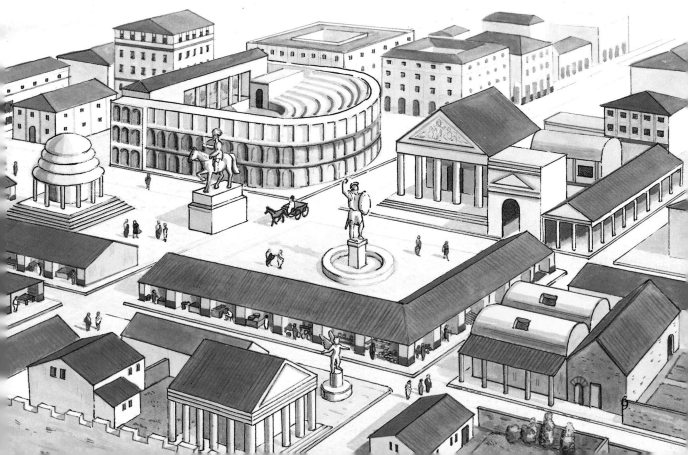

Mosaic picture

Wealthy people decorated their floors with mosaic pictures. Mosaics were made with tiny pieces of colored stone.

You will need:

Cardboard   Glue   Pencil

Scissors   Construction paper in several colors

Follow the steps . . .

1. Draw the outline of a picture on the cardboard.

2. Draw a simple pattern around the edge.

3. Cut construction paper into small squares.

4. Glue the squares inside your pencil outline to make a colorful mosaic.

The Roman army

The strength of the mighty Roman Empire depended on its army. The Roman army conquered new lands, protected the empire against its enemies, and kept the peace.

Roman soldiers had to walk to every corner of the empire. As they went, they built thousands of miles of roads.

Soldiers trained hard every day. Three times a month they practiced marching nineteen miles at a very fast pace. They wore their armor as they marched. They carried their shield, weapons, leg-protectors, and a heavy pack of tools and food.

Life was hard, but they were paid well. When they retired, they were given money or a small plot of land.

A Roman soldier

A foot soldier wore a helmet, a metal vest, an apron of metal-studded straps, and strong sandals.

You will need:

Cardboard   Aluminum foil   Pencil

Red crepe paper   Brown paper   Paint

Scissors   Glue

Follow the steps . . .

1. Paint the outline of a soldier on the cardboard. Cut these shapes for the helmet.

2. Cut strips of:
   – red paper for the tunic
   – foil for the vest
   – brown paper for the apron
   Make balls of aluminum foil for the apron.

3. Glue everything onto your soldier outline.

A Roman standard

A group of eighty soldiers was called a century.

Each century had an emblem called a standard.

You will need:

Cardboard

Red crepe paper

Adhesive tape

Aluminum foil

Scissors

2 cardboard tubes

White glue

Crayons

Pencil

Follow the steps . . .

1. Copy these shapes on the cardboard. Cut them out. Color the sun yellow.

2. Wrap the other shapes in aluminum foil. Press them flat. Tape the cardboard tubes together.

3. Cut strips of cardboard. Glue the foil shapes to the strips. Glue the strips to tube.

4. Glue crepe-paper ribbons onto the rectangle. Add a red fringe to the semicircle.

A shield and sword

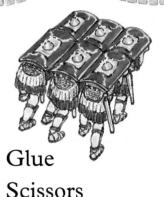

Soldiers could hold their shields together like this to make a protective shell.

You will need:

Cardboard box   Cardboard   Glue

Gold paint   Adhesive tape   Scissors

Red paint   Paintbrush

Follow the steps . . .

1. Cut out the base of the box and paint it red. Paint some cardboard gold.

2. Cut a rectangle and arrows out of gold cardboard. Glue onto the shield. Decorate the edges.

3. Decorate your shield. Glue a circle of gold cardboard onto the center of the shield.

4. Make a handle from cardboard. Tape to back of shield. Cut a sword.

A visit to the baths

Roman people enjoyed going to the baths.
It was a place to meet friends, play games, and relax. Men and women went at different times. Children were allowed in free.

Visitors left their clothes in a cloakroom and went for a cold dip in the *frigidarium*. Next they went into the *tepidarium* for a warm dip.

After that they went into the hot and steamy *caldarium*. It made them sweat. When they came out, olive oil was rubbed into their skin and scraped off with a *strigil*. Finally, they jumped into the cold pool to cool off.

The bath water was heated by large fires under the floor.

Roman numerals

You can write Roman numerals using only these seven letters as building blocks:

I	V	X	L	C	D	M
1	5	10	50	100	500	1000

You will need:

Pencil   Paper

Follow the steps . . .

1. Practice making different Roman numerals by combining the numbers above.

2. To write a big number, add on each part of the number, starting with the highest. For example: 1776 is MDCCLXXVI. M (1000), DCC (500+100+100), LXX (50+10+10), VI (5+1).

3. Read the date in the photograph. The answer is upside down at the bottom.

4. Try writing down the year of your birth.

To count from 1 to 20 in Roman numerals, add or subtract letters like this:

I	II	III	IV	V	VI	VII	VIII	IX	X
1	1+1	1+1+1	5-1	5	5+1	5+1+1	5+1+1+1	10-1	10

XI	XII	XIII	XIV	XV	XVI	XVII	XVIII	XIX	XX
10+1	10+1+1	10+1+1+1	10+(5-1)	10+5	10+5+1	10+5+1+1	10+5+1+1+1	10+(10-1)	10+10

Count by tens like this

X	XX	XXX	XL	L	LX	LXX	LXXX	XC	C
10	10+10	10+10+10	50-10	50	50+10	50+10+10	50+10+10+10	100-10	100

1976

INDEX

Entries in *italics* are activity pages.

amphitheater, 8
army, 12-13

baths, public, 8,
    20-21
brooches, 6
buildings, 8-9

children, 20
citizens, 3
courtyard, 9

emperor, 3
entertainment, 8

floors, 10, 21
food, 13
fountains, 9
friends, 20

games, 20
gates, 8
gods, 8

helmet, 14
houses, 9

lands, 12, 13

map, 2
marketplaces, 8
meals, 9
men, 20
mosaic picture, 10

olive oil, 21

Remus, 2
roads, 8, 12
Roman Empire, 3, 12

Roman numerals, 22
Roman soldier, 14
Roman standard, 16
Rome, 2
Romulus, 2

sandals, 4
slaves, 3
snake bracelet, 6
sword and shield, 18

temples, 8
theater, 8
Tiber River, 2
tools, 13
town, 8-9

water, 9
weapons, 13
women, 20

1995 Childrens Press Edition
© 1995 Watts Books, London, New York, Sydney
All rights reserved. Printed in Malaysia.
Published simultaneously in Canada.
1 2 3 4 5 R 99 98 97 96 95 94

Series Editor: Annabel Martin
Consultant: Richard Tames
Design: Mike Davis
Artwork: Cilla Eurich and Ruth Levy
Photographs: Peter Millard

Library of Congress Cataloging-in-Publication Data:

Hewitt, Sally.
    The Romans / by Sally Hewitt ; illustrated by
Cilla Eurich and Ruth Levy.
        p. cm. – (Footsteps in Time)
        ISBN 0-516-08058-X
        1. Rome–Juvenile literature. [1. Rome.]
    I. Eurich, Cilla. ill.   II. Levy, Ruth, ill.   III. Title.
    IV. Series: Footsteps in Time (Chicago, Ill.)
    DG63.H46 1995   94-42246
    937–dc20   CIP
                                                 AC